American Sign Language

Days and Times

by E. Russell Primm III • illustrated by Kathleen Petelinsek

childsworld.com

The Child's World
childsworld.com

Published by The Child's World®
800-599-READ • childsworld.com

Photography Credits
Krakenimages.com/Shutterstock.com, cover; superelaks/Shutterstock.com, 1, 4; gd_project/Shutterstock.com, 3; kuzmaphoto/Shutterstock.com, 5; Maxim Khytra/Shutterstock.com, 6; Maren Winter/Shutterstock.com, 7; Firuza39/Shutterstock.com, 8; Allexxandar/Shutterstock.com, 9; Jacob_09/Shutterstock.com, 10; Virrage Images/Shutterstock.com, 11; Nadya Kubik/Shutterstock.com, 12; Brian A Jackson/Shutterstock.com, 13; paikong/Shutterstock.com, 14; JLStock/Shutterstock.com, 15; Jamen Percy/Shutterstock.com, 16; ESB Professional/Shutterstock.com, 17; Gabrielle photographs/Shutterstock.com, 18; Monkey Business Images/Shutterstock.com, 19; NASA images/Shutterstock.com, 20; Janthiwa Sutthiboriban/Shutterstock.com, 21

ISBN Information
9781503888999 (Reinforced Library Binding)
9781503890077 (Portable Document Format)
9781503891319 (Online Multi-user eBook)
9781503892552 (Electronic Publication)

LCCN 2023950366

Printed in the United States of America

BRINGING THE WORLD 19 68 TO YOUNG READERS

Note to Parents, Caregivers, and Educators: The understanding of any language begins with the acquisition of vocabulary, whether the language is spoken or manual. The books in this series provide readers, both young and old, with basic American Sign Language signs. Combining close photo cues and simple, but detailed, line illustrations, children and adults alike can begin the process of learning American Sign Language.

Let these books be an introduction to the world of American Sign Language. Most languages have regional dialects and multiple ways of expressing the same thought. This is also true for sign language. We have attempted to use the most common version of the signs for the words in this series. As with any language, the best way to learn is to be taught in person by a frequent user. It is our hope that this series will pique your interest in sign language.

A special thanks to our advisers: As a member of a deaf family that spans four generations, **Kim Bianco Majeri** lives, works, and plays among the Deaf community. **Carmine L. Vozzolo** is an educator of children who are deaf and hard of hearing, as well as their families.

E. Russell Primm III was a well-known figure in the publishing industry who produced thousands of acclaimed books for children. He was affiliated with organizations such as the American Library Association, the Chicago Book Clinic, and the University of Chicago Publishing Program Advisory Board.

Kathleen Petelinsek has loved books since she was a child. Through the years, she has written, designed, and illustrated many books for children. She lives in Wisconsin, near her granddaughter who also shares her love for books.

You can count seconds with a stopwatch. There are 60 seconds in one minute.

Second

Spell S-E-C with your fingers.

The long hand on this clock shows the minutes. There are 60 minutes in one hour.

Minute

Move your right hand forward (one "tick"), as if it were the minute hand on a clock.

Hour

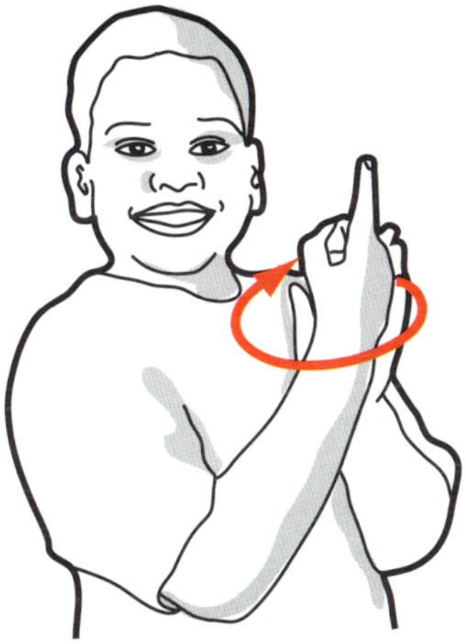

Make the "L" shape with your right hand. Touch the pinky-side of your right hand to your open left hand. Move your right hand in a circle until you end up in the starting position.

The sign for morning is like the sun coming up.

Morning

Place your flat left hand inside your right elbow. Move your flat right hand toward your face.

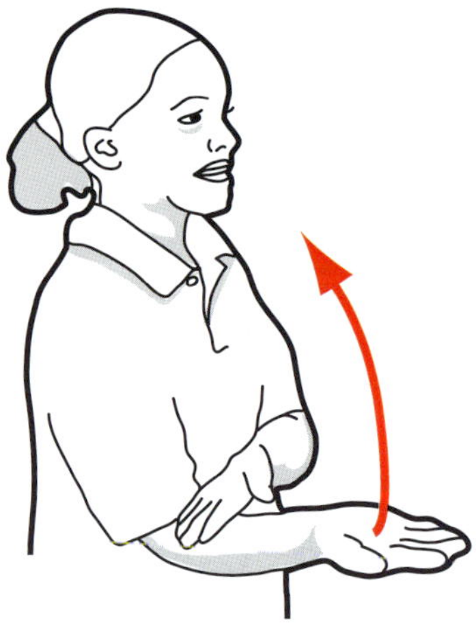

The sign for afternoon is like the sun moving across the sky.

Afternoon

Make both of your hands flat. Angle your right arm out and away from your body. Touch your left index finger to your right elbow.

There are 365 days in one year.

Day

Make the "L" shape with your right hand. Go from pointing straight up to touching your left arm.

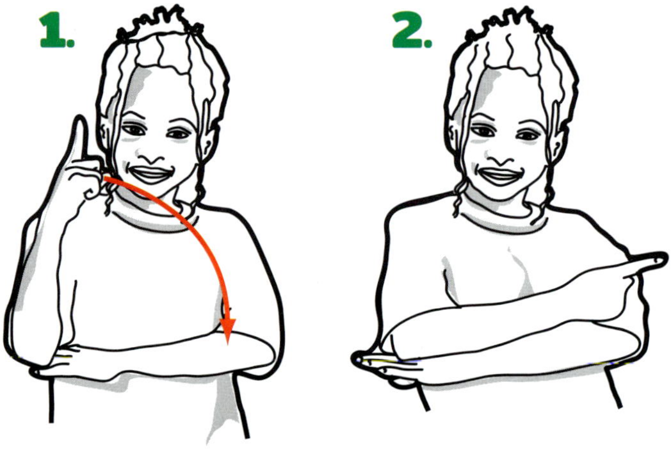

Night

Make both of your hands flat. Put your right wrist over your left. Bend your right wrist.

Early

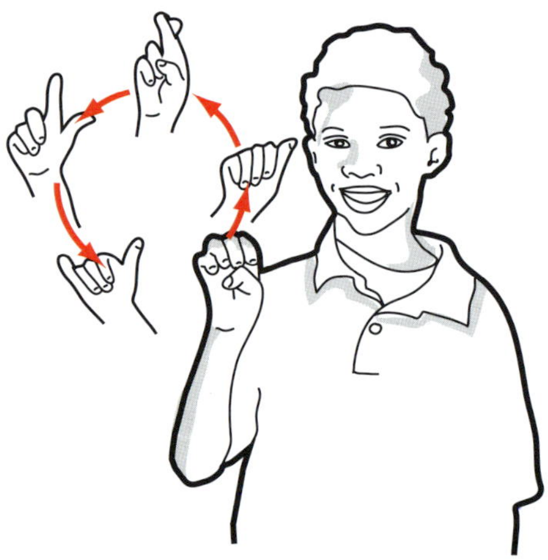

Spell E-A-R-L-Y with your fingers as you move your hand clockwise.

Late is from an Old English word meaning "slow."

Late

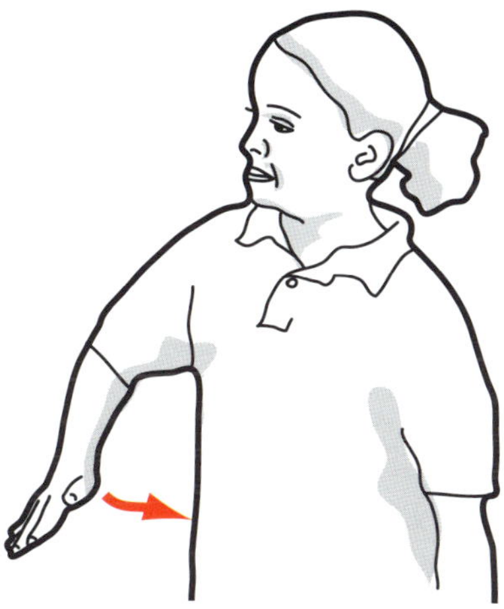

Bend your right arm at your elbow. Push your flat right hand backward—as if you are pushing something behind you.

Some people wear a watch to tell the time.

Time

Tap your wrist a few times as if you are tapping a watch.

1.

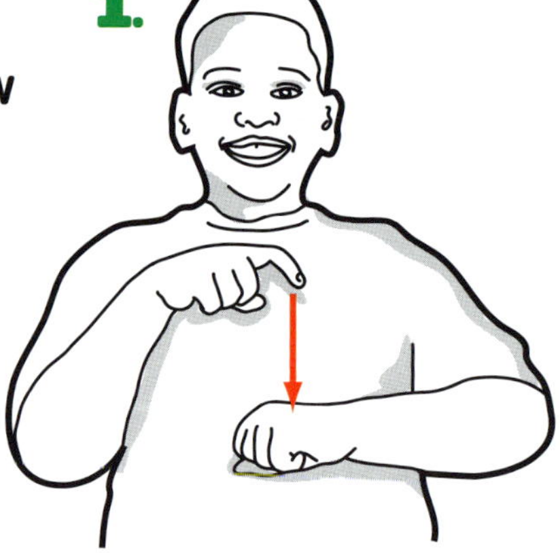

2.

There are 52 weeks in one year.

Week

1. 2.

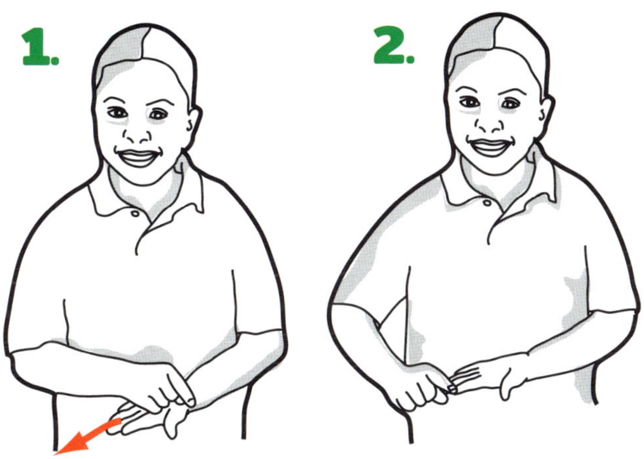

Make the "1" sign with your right hand. Slide it off your left hand.

Many people consider Sunday to be the first day of the week.

Sunday

Face your hands forward. Move both hands in, up, and out in a circle.

Monday comes from an old word meaning "moon day."

Monday

Make the "M" shape with your right hand, facing toward you. Move your hand in circles.

Tuesday is named after the Nordic god Tyr.

Tuesday

Make the "T" shape with your right hand facing toward you. Move your hand in circles.

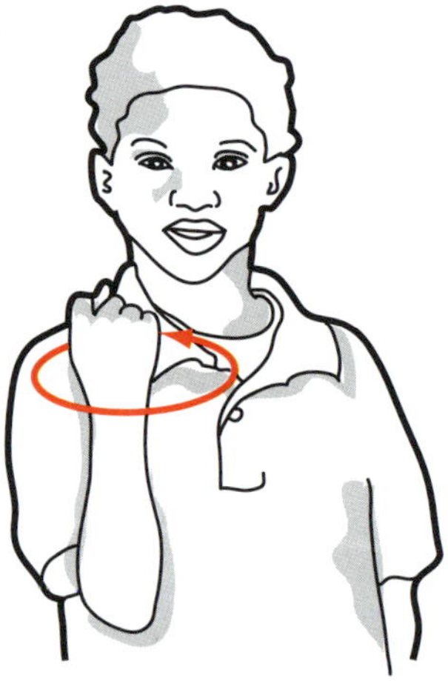

Wednesday is the middle of the work and school week.

Wednesday

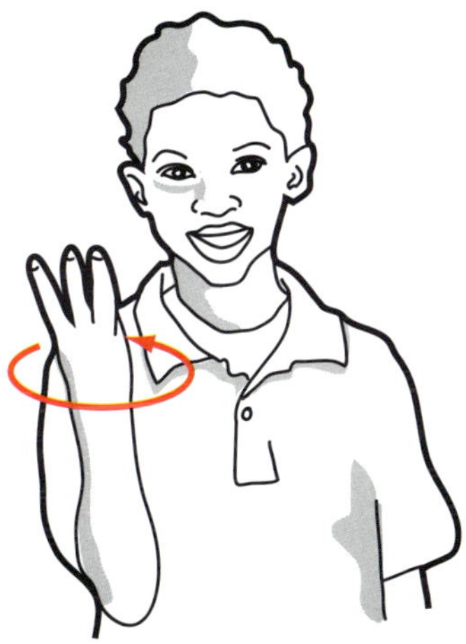

Make the "W" shape with your right hand facing toward you. Move your hand in circles.

Thursday comes from an old word meaning "Thor's Day."

Thursday

Make the "T" shape with your right hand. Then the "H" shape. Repeat.

1.

2.

Many people like Friday. It is the beginning of the weekend.

Friday

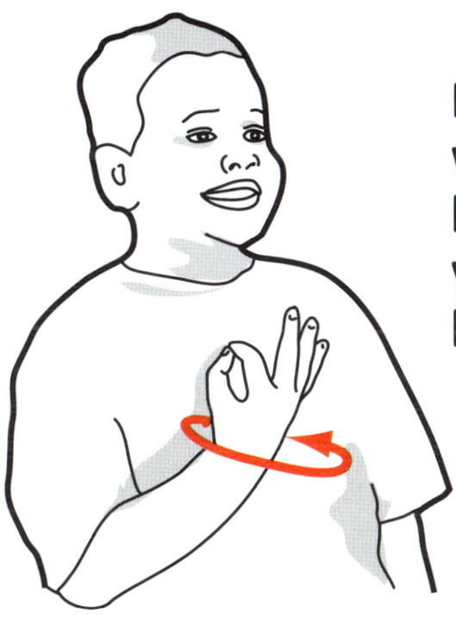

Make the "F" shape with your right hand facing toward you. Move your hand in circles.

Saturday is named after the planet Saturn, which was named after a Roman god called Saturn.

Saturday

Make the "S" shape with your right hand facing toward you. Move your hand in circles.

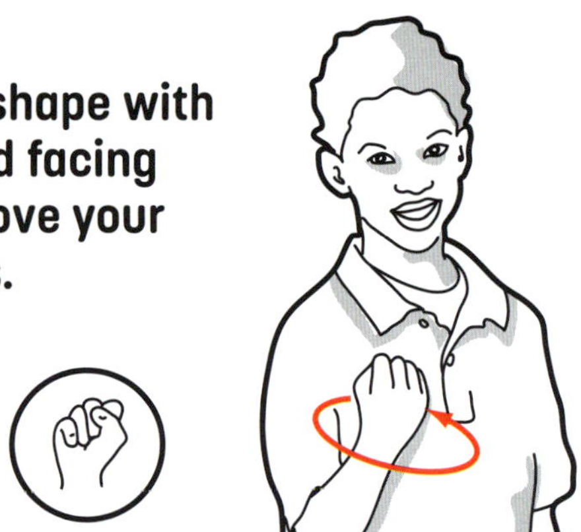

There are 12 months in one year.

Month

1.

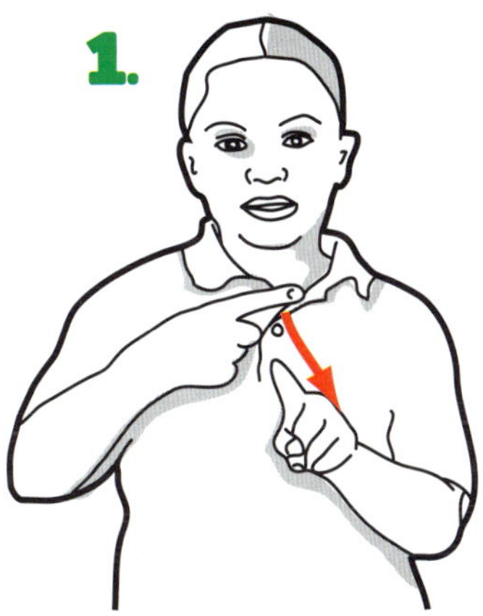

2.

Both hands make the "1" sign. Your left hand points up and stays still. Your right index finger points left and slides down once.

Wonder More

- How much did you know about American Sign Language (ASL) before reading this book? Do you already know some ASL signs? What new signs did you learn?

- Some words or specific names don't have signs. In these cases, you can spell the individual letters of the word, which is called fingerspelling. Look at the alphabet chart on page 23. Can you sign the letters in your name?

- With a partner, pick three signs from this book and practice them together. Are you able to understand each other? Is ASL easier or harder than you thought it would be?

- Think of a day or time word that isn't included in this book. Try signing the word with fingerspelling. Then look up the ASL sign for the word. Where can you find more ASL signs?

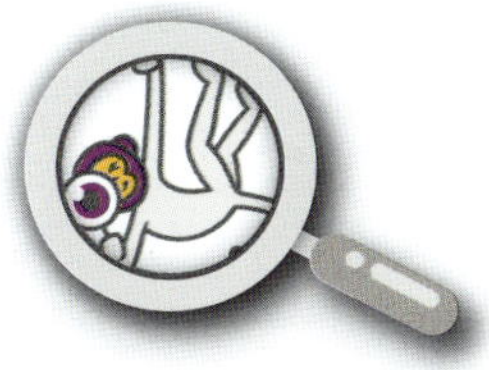

Sign Language Alphabet

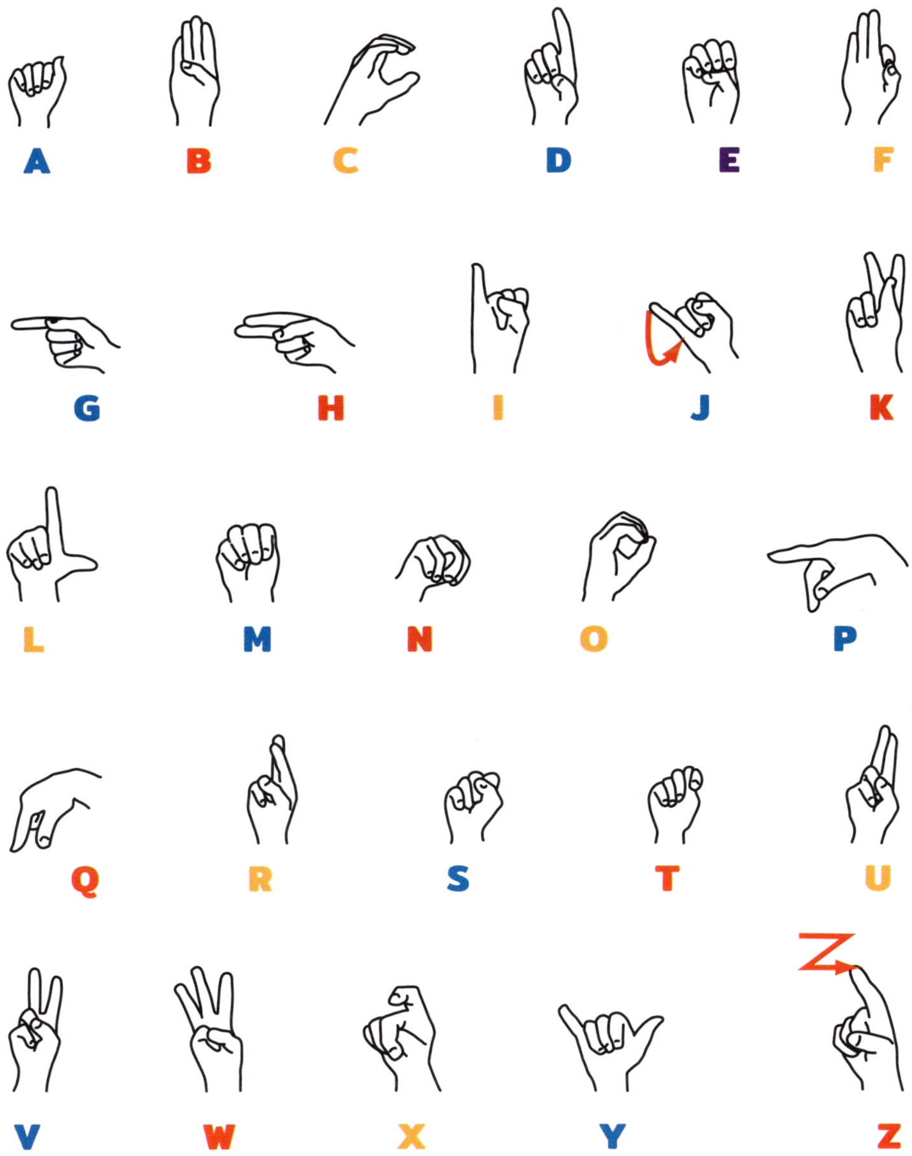

Find Out More

In the Library

Adams, Tara, and Natalia Sanabria (illustrator). *We Can Sign! An Essential Guide to American Sign Language for Kids*. Emeryville, CA: Rockridge Press, 2020.

Martin, Ann M., and Chan Chau (illustrator). *Jessi's Secret Language: A Graphic Novel (The Baby-Sitters Club Graphix)*. New York, NY: Scholastic, 2022.

On the Web

Visit our website for links about American Sign Language:

childsworld.com/links

Note to Parents, Caregivers, Teachers, and Librarians: We routinely verify our web links to make sure they are safe and active sites. So encourage your readers to check them out!

A Special Thank-You!

Thank you to our models from the Program for Children Who are Deaf and Hard of Hearing at the Alexander Graham Bell School in Chicago, Illinois.

Alina's favorite things to do are art, soccer, and swimming. DJ is her brother!

Darionna likes the swings and merry-go-round on the playground. She also loves art.

Dareous likes football. His favorite team is the Detroit Lions. He also likes to play video games.

DJ loves playing the harmonica and video games. Alina is his sister!